China Fiscal Policy Revamp Faces Hurdles

Iacob Koch-Weser

During his first year in office, President Xi Jinping put fiscal reform back on top of China's policy agenda. The Party Politburo followed the president's lead in June, promising to finish major fiscal and tax reform tasks by 2016 and establish a modern fiscal system by 2020.[1] Among the proposals is the elimination of a tax that discriminates against services companies, adding a recurring tax on property, and imposing a price-based tax on coal, along with measures to improve budget management.

China last overhauled its tax-and-spend system in 1994, when the country's economy was much smaller and its accession to the World Trade Organization was in doubt. The economy took off in the ensuing years, but the fiscal system remained largely unaltered. Fiscal reform in the world's second-largest economy now carries significant implications for U.S. businesses and the world economy.

Why now? Finance Minister Lou Jiwei, after six years as Chairman of China Investment Corporation (China's sovereign wealth fund), wants to make his mark as a reformer. The government is also facing gaps in the budget. An audit commissioned last fall by Premier Li Keqiang revealed local governments across the country are mired in debt that will soon mature and must either be rolled over or retired with new revenue.

Aside from scoring political points and plugging budget gaps, fiscal reform could

Key Points

- Since its last overhaul in 1994, China's flawed fiscal system has muddled through. Local debt, slowing revenue, and greater spending obligations are now spurring a new round of reform under President Xi Jinping.
- By eliminating the so-called "business tax," Beijing is allowing services companies to enjoy the same tax deductions and rebates manufacturers do. The government may also establish a price-based tax on coal and a recurring tax on property.
- The government ultimately seeks to rebalance the economy. Fiscal reform could boost services, prevent housing bubbles, redistribute income, and reduce pollution. But it will be difficult to implement in China's segmented economy and authoritarian system.
- The central government has a clear vision for improving budget flexibility and transparency. Yet it remains ambivalent about how to share revenue, spending responsibilities, and borrowing authority with local governments.

address structural issues. China's provincial and municipal system is eroding. The central government runs a budget surplus, but local governments rely on shady borrowing, land sales, and other off-budget revenues to make up for shortfalls. The tax burden is unevenly

1

distributed—to the advantage of state-owned enterprises (SOEs) and the elite, but to the detriment of small businesses and the emerging consumer class. China's fiscal problems add to those in the real economy, where inequality is rising, environmental costs are mounting, and growth is tied to property investment and industrial output.

This issue brief argues that, slowly but surely, China is adopting a new fiscal paradigm. President Xi seeks to "kill two birds with one stone," fixing the fiscal system as a means to rebalance the economy. Even as China maintains a "state-capitalist" system, it is keen to tax and spend as progressively as a wealthy market economy. However, technical barriers and conflicts of interest are likely to delay and dilute fiscal reform. Coal and property taxes could destabilize the economy. Powerful SOEs oppose corporate tax reforms in strategic sectors, and ordinary households complain their tax burden is heavy enough as it is. Beijing also faces a delicate balancing act between devolving budgetary authority to local officials, and exerting sufficient control to prevent waste and mismanagement.

The Erosion of China's Fiscal System

The Legacy of the 1994 Fiscal Reform

China's 1994 tax overhaul, implemented in the early years of President Jiang Zemin's tenure, had practical intentions. The central government sought to rein in the autonomy of local governments, which collected the bulk of the nation's taxes, borrowed from local banks, and kept separate books for off-budget expenses. The consequences of poor fiscal management were painfully evident in many developing countries that suffered a "lost decade" of debt in the 1980s. Beijing was also wary of the gaps in fiscal power between coastal and inland regions, and the blurred division between central and local spending.

The 1994 tax reforms adopted several measures to address these issues:

- *Balanced budgets and borrowing restrictions.* Beijing required local governments to keep their annual fiscal deficits below a certain threshold. It also gave the central government a monopoly over domestic and foreign borrowing, so local governments could not plug budget gaps by issuing bonds.[2]
- *Revenue-sharing and transfers.* The tax code was revised, giving the central government sole or dominant authority over important tax items. The largest of the shared taxes is the value-added tax (VAT), newly created in 1994 and split 75-25 between central and local authorities. The goal was for the central government to collect 60 percent of the nation's overall tax revenues and make 40 percent of the expenditures in order to transfer its 20 percent budget surplus to less-developed regions.[3]
- *Clarifying expenditure obligations.* The central government assumed all spending on national defense, diplomacy and armed forces, and national infrastructure projects, leaving most other areas—including urban construction, education, and healthcare—to the subnational budgets.[4]

Reasonable on paper, the 1994 tax overhaul has not worked as well in practice. To begin, fiscal redistribution has been limited, contributing to large income gaps among provinces (see Table 1). In China's five-tier fiscal system, the funds disbursed from the center to localities tend to get stuck at the provincial level, trickling down piecemeal to municipalities, counties, and townships. Of China's 28 tax categories, the 18 earmarked to local governments provide meager revenues or are difficult to collect, while the larger, more stable taxes (e.g., the VAT and enterprise income tax) are shared with the central government.[5] At the same time, lower-level governments shoulder an inordinate share of spending on public services.

Table 1: Per Capita Income Differences across Provinces/States: China vs. United States (ratios)

	China		United States	
	2005	2012	2005	2012
Top : Bottom	2.46	2.42	1.87	1.78
Top5 : Bottom5	2.03	1.95	1.62	1.59
Top10 : Bottom10	1.69	1.63	1.47	1.48

Source: China National Bureau of Statistics, via CEIC; U.S Department of Commerce, Bureau of Economic Analysis (March 2013). *https://bber.unm.edu/econ/us-pci.htm*.
Note: "Top : Bottom" refers to the income ratio between the wealthiest and poorest provinces/states. "Top5 : Bottom5 " refers to the ratio between the average per capita income in the five wealthiest and five poorest provinces/states. The same calculation is used for "Top10 : Bottom10." CEIC does not provide data before 2005.

Fiscal irregularities persist as well. Central-local transfers are frequently issued for special purposes, making them ripe for cronyism. Local authorities keep debts off their books and rely on extrabudgetary income from land transfers. Tax evasion is rampant, and collection inefficient; according to one estimate, 10 percent of the value of taxes collected in China goes into the cost of collecting (the rate is 0.5 percent in the United States.) Contributing to this problem are the excessive number of tax items and a balkanized system that separates local from central revenue authorities.[*]

Further, China's fiscal system reflects the priorities of an authoritarian state with a Soviet legacy. China's courts, understaffed and rife with Party interference, barely handle tax cases, giving aggrieved taxpayers limited legal recourse.[†] In the United States, Congress passes tax legislation; in China, only three of the 18 major tax items were passed by legislation. The rest are regulations set by the State Council. Finance Minister Lou has acknowledged that this practice causes irregularities such as "unapproved tax incentives offered by local governments."[6] To the extent that the National People's Congress (NPC) retains fiscal influence, it does so by setting Soviet-style budget targets on an annual basis, counter to the advanced practice of flexible management and forecasting. SOEs enjoy tax breaks and generous subsidies.[‡]

---

[*] The State Administration of Taxation and its local offices are responsible for collecting the VAT and some other taxes attributable to the central government. Local governments have their own institutions responsible for collecting their own revenues, mainly the business tax. *How China Restructures Its Tax System: Q&A with Wei Xiong [Professor of Law at Wuhan University]* (Max Planck Institute for Tax Law and Public Finance, October 2013). *http://www.tax.mpg.de/en/pub/news/chinese_tax_reforms.cfm*.

[†] China's courts are overburdened by civil and commercial cases. According to one estimate, each of China's three thousand courts hears only one tax case every three years because their caseloads are so great. As a result, it is impossible for the courts to develop expertise to deal with tax disputes. Most cases only revolve around the procedural issues for these very limited tax cases. *How China Restructures Its Tax System: Q&A with Wei Xiong [Professor of Law at Wuhan University]* (Max Planck Institute for Tax Law and Public Finance, October 2013). *http://www.tax.mpg.de/en/pub/news/chinese_tax_reforms.cfm*.

[‡] Central SOEs pay a portion of their profits into the "state capital management budget" that is run separately from MOF's budget. Most of those payments get distributed back to the SOEs via research and development (R&D) subsidies and other means. In 2013, of the RMB 106 billion in central SOE dividend payments, just 6 percent went to MOF's general budget. The MOF report submitted to the 2014 NPC meetings suggests local SOEs do not pay dividends into the MOF budget at all. Stephen Green, "Chinese Finance Minister's To-Do List," *China Daily*, March 7, 2014. *http://www.chinadaily.com.cn/business/2014-03/07/content_17331598.htm*.

The imperative to meet output targets has spilled over into the tax code, which primarily incentivizes the industrial sector. Since 1994, manufacturers have paid a VAT that permits them to seek tax deductions for returns on investment and for the cost of intermediate inputs they use in their products. Services providers, on the other hand, have paid a business tax[§] that does not allow for such deductions.[7] There is not much regard for consumer interests, either. China charges excise taxes on a wide range of consumer items, including vehicles—making U.S. cars much pricier in China than in the United States. Imported consumer items carry a heftier price tag than in developed markets, due not only to the artificial devaluation of the renminbi currency, but also high consumption taxes that hit imports disproportionately hard.[**] Meanwhile, the wealthiest Chinese benefit from low taxes on capital gains, property, inheritance, and gifts.[8]

The glitches in China's fiscal system became visible as early as the 1990s. Yet until recently, they did not pose a threat to the Communist regime. On the contrary, the 1994 reforms were a political success for the Party: they strengthened central government spending on the military and, by means of tax-sharing schemes, tied the fate of local Party cadres to central authorities.[9] Another mitigating factor has been rapid economic growth. The losers of the fiscal system—inland regions, rural townships, private and services enterprises, and low-income households—have been assuaged by improvements in business conditions and living standards. To some degree, fiscal decentralization has spurred economic growth by encouraging localities to compete with one another to increase revenues.[10]

Equally important, Beijing has applied a "light touch" to fiscal policy. Taxing and spending take a backseat to the government's monetary intervention (currency, capital, and price controls), industry regulation, corporate ownership, and other policy tools. Data published by the Heritage Foundation in 2012 shows China has one of the lowest tax-to-GDP ratios among the world's large economies, well below the Organization for Economic Cooperation and Development (OECD) average of 34 percent (see Figure 1).[††] According to Nicholas Lardy, an economist at the Peterson Institute for International Economics, only around 8 percent of Chinese households pay income taxes.[11] Household income, which accounts for 46 percent of tax revenue in the United States, comprises just 6 percent in China.[12] As a result, failings in the fiscal system may be less obvious in China than in tax-heavy countries.

[§] China charges three types of turnover taxes: value-added tax (VAT), consumption tax, and business tax. The levy of these taxes normally is based on the volume of business tax or sales of the taxpayers in the manufacturing, circulation, or services sectors. Manufacturers pay the VAT, while services providers pay the business tax.

[**] According to U.S. economist Tom Miller, "Imported goods [in China] are subject to three major levies—import tariffs, VAT and a 'consumption tax'—plus other smaller taxes, often charged locally. Take a tube of lipstick with an import value of Rmb100. After adding the import tariff (10%), VAT (17%), consumption tax (30%) and other local taxes and fees (about 5%), the retailer must sell it for around Rmb200 to make a reasonable profit. Of course, almost all countries charge import tariffs and VAT or sales taxes [...] Where China differs is in charging high consumption taxes on top." Tom Miller, "Screwing the Consumer," *China Economic Quarterly* 17:3 (September 2013): 47.

[††] Other sources cite higher figures. According to one source, China's tax-to-GDP ratio rose from 16 percent in 2003 to 22.7 percent in 2013. Takehiko Nakao [President of Asian Development Bank], "The Road to Public Finance Reform" (Speech delivered at China Development Forum 2014, Beijing, March 23, 2014) reprinted by *China Daily*, March 25, 2014. *http://www.chinadaily.com.cn/business/2014-03/25/content_17377356.htm.*

Figure 1: Tax-to-GDP Ratios among the World's Largest Economies, 2012
(ratio, %)

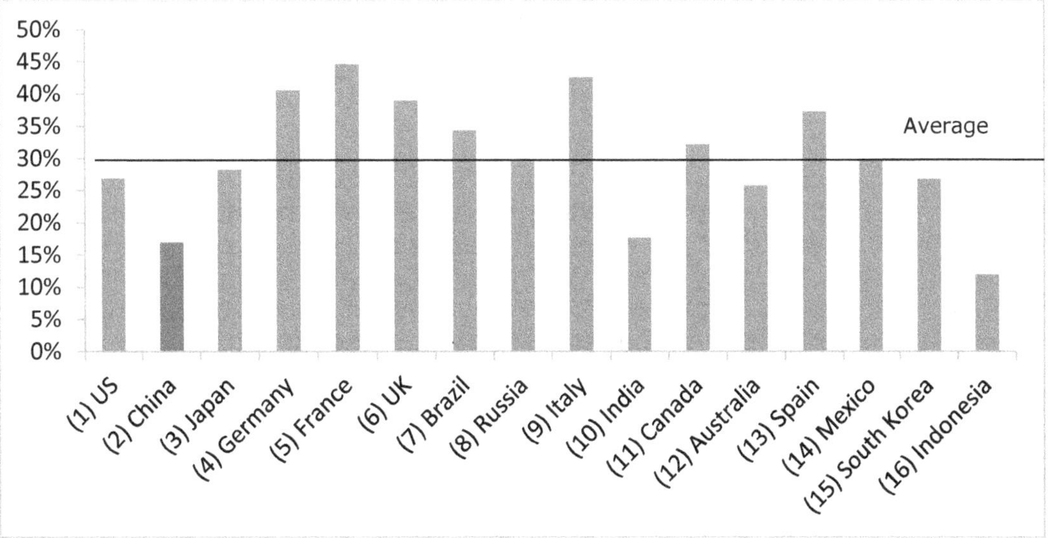

Source: Heritage Foundation.

Mounting Pressure to Reform

Since the 2007–2008 global financial crisis, it has become harder for China's fiscal system to muddle through. Local government debt has metastasized into a systemic risk. The primary culprits are local government financial vehicles (LGFVs)—investment companies that help local governments circumvent official borrowing restrictions. LGFVs use state-owned land as collateral to borrow from banks on the government's behalf, channelling funds into local construction projects that in turn raise the value of land. There are now over 10,000 LGFVs, accounting for approximately 40 percent of local government debt.[13] These companies began to proliferate in 2009, when local governments were ordered by Beijing to shoulder two-thirds of the RMB 4 trillion ($643 billion) economic stimulus package.[14]

The nationwide audit of local debt, released last December, showed the liabilities of China's municipalities rose by nearly 70 percent between 2011 and 2013, reaching some RMB 17.9 trillion ($2.95 trillion)[15]—that compared with a year-end 2010 total of RMB 10.7 trillion ($1.62 trillion) given in an audit office report in June 2011.[16] The audit determined 60 percent of local government debt will mature before the end of 2015.[‡‡] The liabilities are concentrated in municipal (44.5 percent) and county-level (36.4 percent) governments, the worst deprived in terms of fiscal revenue and transfers.[17]

China's top officials have played down the risks. Finance Minister Lou has insisted the chances of local government default are "not great."[18] At the annual meetings of the NPC in March, Premier Li argued that China's overall budget remains in good health and leaves room to expand fiscal spending.[19] Indeed, local debt looks manageable at around 30 percent of GDP.[20] China's official budget deficit, projected by *The Economist* to reach 2.9 percent of

---

‡‡ A 2010 audit stated that more than 50 percent of debt would mature before the end of 2013. The *Financial Times* concluded "the vast majority was not paid back but simply refinanced." Simon Rabinovich, "China Gives Local Government Go-Ahead to Roll Over Debt," *Financial Times*, January 2, 2014. *http://www.ft.com/intl/cms/s/0/055e48f8-7371-11e3-a0c0-00144feabdc0.html#axzz3ELqiDuDk*.

GDP in 2014, is much lower than Japan's 7.8 percent deficit, and roughly on par with the United States and the euro area.[21]

The problem for the government is that local debt is not an isolated problem that can be quarantined. This issue is compounded by (1) imbalances between central and local budgets, (2) the decline in fiscal revenue growth, and (3) social pressure to increase fiscal spending.

Though the central government likes to blame local officials for profligacy and incompetence,[22] the root cause of the debt crisis is the 1994 tax reform. The original vision of China's planners was for local governments to account for 40 percent of national revenue and 60 percent of spending. China's official data suggests that local governments accounted for 85 percent of national spending and 53 percent of revenue in 2013 (see Figure 2.1). This data may contain accounting inconsistencies,[§§] but the trend is clear. The central government has lost its desired control over revenue, while leaving local governments with an onerous spending obligation. To plug this gap, Beijing would have to shift a larger portion of its central budget over to local transfers. Yet the tendency in recent years is the opposite (see Figure 2.2).

Figure 2.1: Growth of China's Central Government Tax Revenue and Expenditure (share, %)

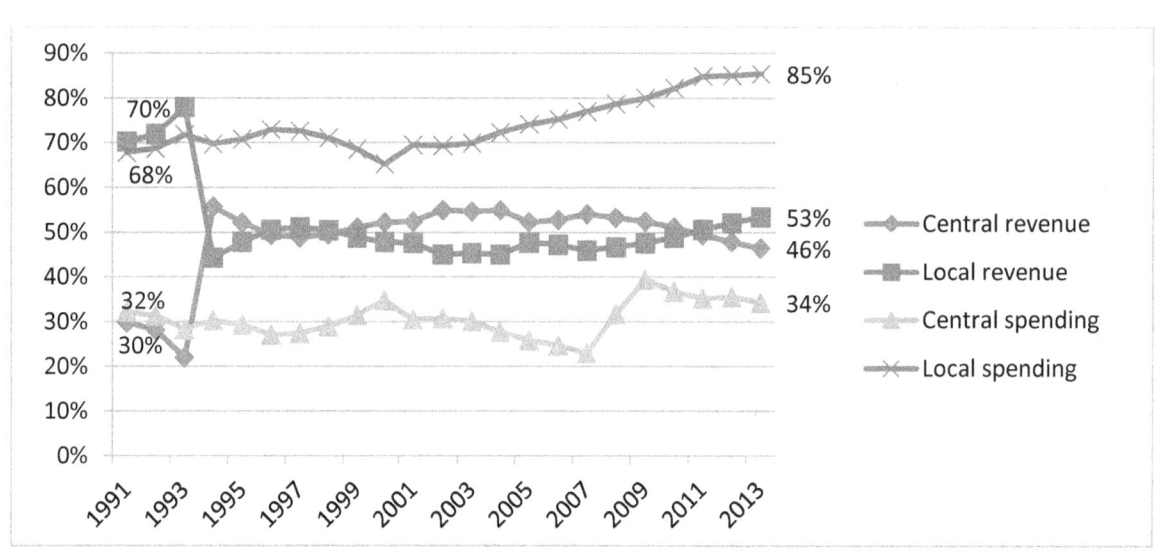

Source: China's Ministry of Finance, via CEIC.
Note: Spending of local and central governments adds up to >100% after 2008.

[§§] There are some inconsistencies in China's taxing and spending data. In 2008, the sum of central and local spending in China's official statistics (aggregated by CEIC) began to exceed 100 percent of total revenue. Moreover, Bloomberg cites the local government revenue share at 40 percent and the spending share at 80 percent. Bloomberg, "China's Local Debt Swells to 17.9 Trillion Yuan in Audit," December 30, 2013. *http://www.bloomberg.com/news/2013-12-30/china-s-local-debt-swells-to-17-9-trillion-yuan-in-audit.html.*

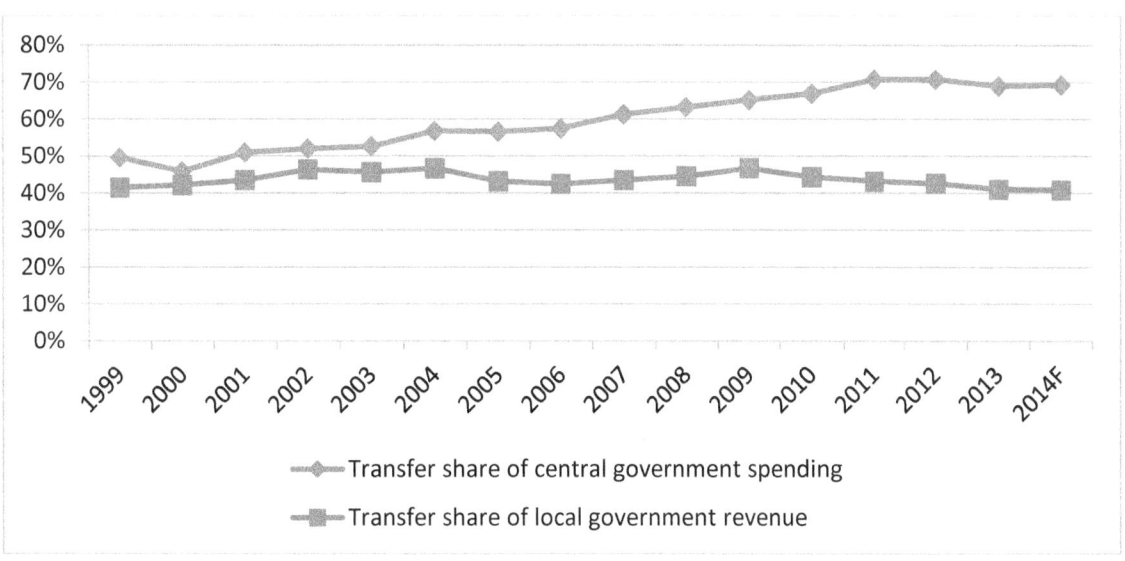

Figure 2.2: Fiscal Transfers and Tax Rebates in China:
As Share of Central Government Spending and Local Government Revenue
(share, %)

Sources: China's Ministry of Finance, via CEIC; China's Ministry of Finance 2014 Work Report.
Note: 2014F refers to 2014 budget forecast.

Concurrently, China's slowing economy has dampened tax revenue. Overall revenue rose by 10.1 percent in 2013, the lowest rate in over a decade (see Figure 3). MOF has forecast revenue growth to slow even further in 2014, to about 8 percent year-on-year. According to Stephen Green, a leading China economist, "Income got so tight early [in 2014] that MOF had to unexpectedly slow some spending, including spending on transfers to local governments."[23] Local government revenue did slightly better, rising by 13 percent in 2013. Still, that was well below the decade average of over 20 percent.[24] The drop is most salient in poorer inland regions; in the first half of 2014, for example, resource-rich Shaanxi Province recorded 12.6 percent growth in tax revenue, down from 26.6 percent a year earlier, largely due to a drop in coal demand. The wealthier coastal regions have held steady, but the key revenue driver is the property market. In Shandong Province, for instance, taxes collected from the housing market contributed 53.7 percent of revenue growth in the first six months of 2014, even though they only make up 17 percent of the revenue base.[25]

Not least, China's changing demographics are putting Beijing under immense pressure to boost fiscal outlays. China's median age will exceed that of the United States within this decade, and the proportion aged 65 and above will increase to 25 percent by 2040, totaling three hundred million.[26] China's urbanization rate—which counts migrants living in cities for over six months as urban residents—surpassed the 50 percent mark in 2011.[27] Already, the government is undertaking legal and policy reforms that will weigh down government finances for years to come. Healthcare reforms over the past ten years have expanded public health insurance from near zero to some 95 percent of China's population.[28] At the Third Plenary Session of the 18th Party Congress (Third Plenum), held in November 2013, China's leadership announced that it would relax urban residency permits (*hukou*) to give the country's migrant workers expanded access to urban amenities.[***]

[***] The government proposes to relax migrants' ability to get urban residence permits under strict government supervision: "Open up the restrictions on settlement in organizational towns [*jianzhi zhen*] and small cities, open

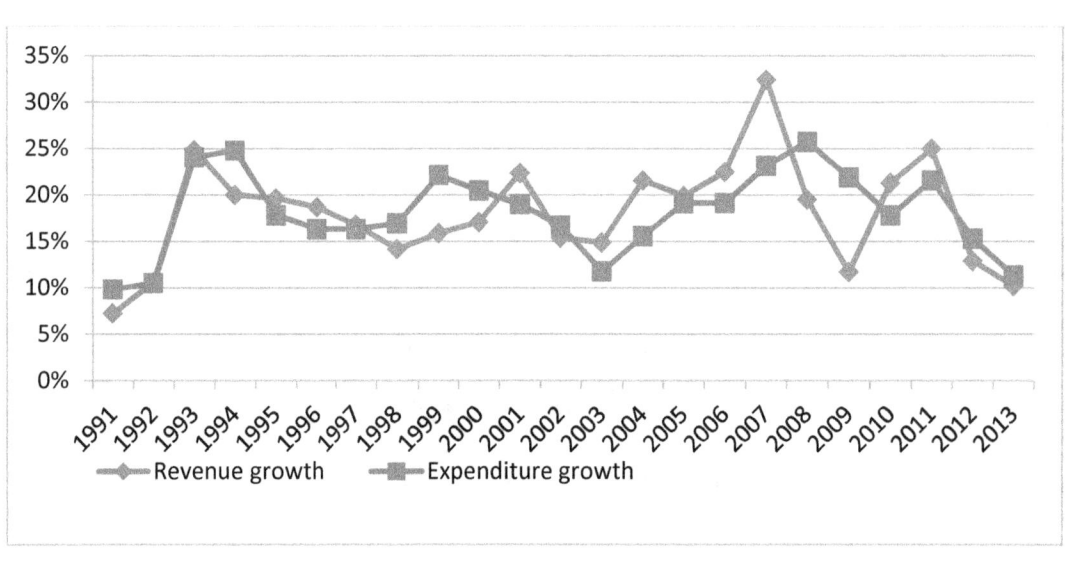

Figure 3: Growth of China's Government Tax Revenue and Expenditure (year-on-year, %)

Source: China's Ministry of Finance, via CEIC.

Adjusting China's Tax Code

Combining Fiscal Reform with Economic Rebalancing

Faced with fiscal challenges, China's leadership is changing tack. The Third Plenum Decision contains a section on "deepening fiscal reform" that lays out several progressive concepts, including improving budget management, changing the composition of tax revenue and incentives, and reconfiguring central-local spending obligations. The Decision further states:

> *Financial administration is the foundation and important pillar of state governance and a scientific fiscal and taxation system is the institutional guarantee for optimizing resource allocation, safeguarding market unity, promoting social fairness and achieving long-term peace and stability.*[29]

The momentum of the Third Plenum Decision has carried over into 2014. Although China's fiscal spending is slowing along with revenue, MOF announced in March it would adopt a "proactive fiscal stance" in 2014.[30] Healthcare and social security are among the fastest growing items in this year's budget.[31] While local government revenue growth slowed in the first half of 2014, expenditure increased significantly because local governments are required by Beijing to increase their input into healthcare, education, and other sectors.[32]

---

up in orderly fashion the restrictions on settlement in medium-sized cities, rationally set the conditions for settlement in large cities, and strictly control the population scale in very large cities." For more details, see Nargiza Salidjanova and Iacob Koch-Weser, *Third Plenum Economic Reform Proposals: A Scorecard* (U.S.-China Economic and Security Review Commission, November 19, 2013). *http://origin.www.uscc.gov/sites/default/files/Research/Backgrounder_Third%20Plenum%20Economic%20Reform %20Proposals--A%20Scorecard%20%282%29.pdf*.

China's "state-capitalist" economy remains far removed from the tax-and-spend politics of a wealthy market economy. Even so, the leadership appears keen to "kill two birds with one stone," fixing the nation's finances as a means to rebalance the economy. Western economists have advocated as much for years. In a 2012 op-ed published in *China Daily*, Asian Development Bank economists Robert Wihtol and Yolanda Fernandez Lommen state:

> *Three decades of fast growth have transformed China into the world's second largest economy. They have also created an economy that is excessively reliant on investment, exports and capital-intensive industrial development, and in pressing need of rebalancing [. . .] In developed economies, large fiscal transfers, for healthcare, education and pensions, have effectively reduced inequality. Reforms to broaden the tax base and increase the progressivity of taxation were also successful in redistributing incomes [. . .] Looking ahead, policymaking for China's next-generation leaders should focus on overhauling taxation and fiscal transfers to balance income distribution.* [33]

Of all the various fiscal reforms on the table, the leadership is moving fastest on the tax code.[34] The major changes being considered are:

- *Taxing services and industry equally.* This is the most advanced of China's tax reforms. The idea is to eliminate the business tax—charged by local governments on the revenue of services providers—in favor of the VAT charged on the industrial sector (the "B2V" reform). The change will allow services companies to deduct not only revenues they earn from making investments, but also the cost of purchasing intermediate inputs. It will also make them eligible for the VAT rebates the government offers to goods exporters. B2V reforms were piloted in Shanghai as of January 2012, and expanded nationwide in August 2013. However, not all services sectors have been included. The objective is to extend the reform to rail, post, and telecommunications companies by year-end 2014. The big exceptions are finance, real estate, and construction. Finance Minister Lou expects the B2V reform to be complete by year-end 2015.[35]
- *Increasing taxes on resources and polluting activities.* The government has promised a litany of environment-related taxes designed to discourage polluting activities and to generate revenue to clean them up. This could involve an environmental protection tax that would convert local pollutant discharge fees into a national tax, extending the existing resource tax to cover more products (e.g., agrochemicals) or increasing excise taxes on energy-intensive products (building on the 2009 excise tax on automotive fuel). The preliminary goal for 2014, though, is to convert the resource tax on coal from a quantity- to a value-based tax.[36] Coal is an abundant and cheap input that accounts for two-thirds of China's energy mix. Ad valorem taxes on oil and gas, enacted in 2011, led to a 67 percent revenue jump.[37]
- *Increasing taxes on property.* China already levies numerous taxes on property, predominantly at the local level. The government is proposing a shift from transaction-based taxes to one recurring tax (a.k.a., "real estate tax"), as is common practice in advanced economies. The tax will be assessed based on a property's current market value instead of its (lower) historic value. The new property tax could help reduce speculation by increasing the annual "holding" costs of homeownership. Property tax pilots were carried out on a subset of luxury properties in Shanghai and Chongqing beginning in 2012. At the March NPC meetings, however, the government provided few details, other than reiterating the Third Plenum Decision to "accelerate property tax legislation."[38]
- *Increasing taxes on private wealth.* In addition to a property tax, the government is seeking other ways to tax personal wealth. In his presentation in May at a Beijing

conference attended by Chinese officials, U.S. economist Ryan Rutkowski suggested China could lower the threshold for taxpayer eligibility for the personal income tax by up to 80 percent and still be in line with International Monetary Fund (IMF) standards for optimizing redistribution of personal income. China could also raise its top income tax rate from 45 percent to 60 percent.[39] Alternatively, the base for assessing personal income tax could be expanded to include nonwage income. This could be combined with a higher capital gains tax rate (currently below the tax rate on wages) or the creation of an inheritance tax. In contrast to the other taxes outlined above, there has been little movement on private wealth taxes thus far. The Third Plenum Decision vaguely states China should adopt a "comprehensive" personal income tax (presumably including nonwage income).[40]

If done right, a revised tax code could constrain harmful and reward beneficial economic activities. The revision could come back to benefit the fiscal system by raising revenues and reducing externalities (e.g., pollution and illness) that compound fiscal liabilities. Like the 1994 reforms, however, what looks good on the face of things does not necessarily succeed in China's segmented economy and authoritarian system.

Taxing Businesses: Maintaining Revenue and Trumping SOEs

In the United States, corporations contribute only a small piece of the national tax pie. The corporate income tax share of revenue was 9.9 percent in 2013, well below its postwar average of 15.8 percent. In comparison, household income and social security contributions, taken together, accounted for 81.6 percent of U.S. revenue that year. In China's fiscal system, companies play a greater role: enterprise income accounted for 20 percent of revenue in 2013, and business tax (levied on services providers) accounted for 16 percent. The largest tax revenue driver is the VAT that Chinese industrial producers pay at every stage of production—a tax that ultimately falls on the consumer. The VAT does not exist in the United States, although many states have sales taxes, which are similar (see Figures 4.1 and 4.2).

Corporate taxes are no longer rising significantly as a share of China's tax revenue. Indeed, the VAT share has declined precipitously since its peak in the mid-1990s. The national tax base, already quite fragmented, depends increasingly on land-based transactions tied to the property market, as well as regressive consumer taxes. The government therefore faces a delicate balancing act, ensuring corporate taxes remain a staple of the tax regime while also pursuing market-based tax reforms that reduce the burden on up-and-coming enterprises.

The 2008 corporate income tax reform marked an important step in this direction. The government revised a 1991 law that allowed foreign-invested enterprises (FIEs) to pay at a preferential rate. It introduced a new, uniform 25 percent taxation rate at a midpoint between the 15 percent rate FIEs paid and the 33 percent rate tax domestic firms paid.[41] The reform achieved its desired effect on revenue: between 2008 and 2013, enterprise income tax increased its share of national tax revenue by 1.5 percent, after declining by 8.6 percent over the previous 15 years.[42]

Figure 4.1: Composition of China's Fiscal Revenue
(share, %)

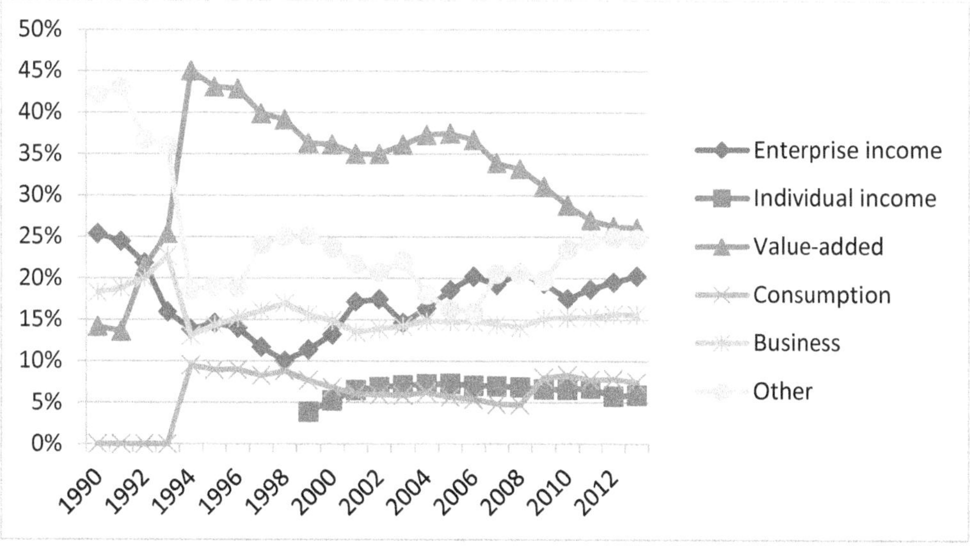

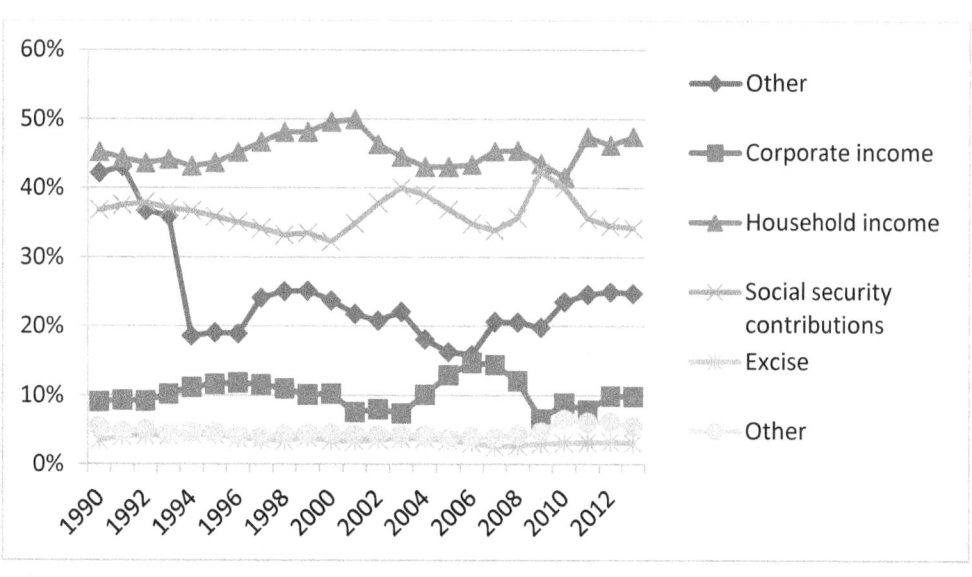

Source: China's Ministry of Finance, via CEIC.

Figure 4.2: Composition of U.S. Fiscal Revenue
(share, %)

Source: Office of Management and Budget, Historical Tables, via Tax Policy Center.
http://www.taxpolicycenter.org/taxfacts/displayafact.cfm?Docid=203.

Replacing the business tax with a VAT (B2V reform) marks a new phase in corporate tax reform because it levels the playing field for services providers. Various companies seem to favor the change. In areas where the reform has been implemented, larger manufacturers that previously kept in-house transport and logistics subsidiaries for tax purposes are spinning off these units and outsourcing to specialized services providers, so as to focus on their core business. Services firms, meanwhile, are reinvesting a larger share of revenue and looking to export in order to take advantage of VAT rebates.[43] B2V reform is certain to decrease the tax burden on services companies. China's tax authorities estimate the nationwide tax burden was cut by about RMB 140 billion ($22.4 billion) by the end of 2013 due to B2V.[44] The government's calculus is that a larger services sector will eventually increase its share of the corporate tax base, even as the proportional burden on each company decreases.

The staunchest opponents of eliminating the business tax are China's oligopolistic, state-owned services providers. These companies rely less on deductibles and rebates the VAT would offer, and prefer the business tax for its lower tax rate. In June 2014, China's three major telecommunications operators cried foul, claiming the elimination of the business tax would eat into their profits.[†††] This did not discourage MOF from canceling the business tax in the telecommunications sector. The state-dominated financial sector, however, is a different story. Banks currently pay the business tax at a rate of 5 percent, versus the VAT rate of 11 percent. In addition, B2V reform in the financial sector is projected to increase the number of transactions, which will pose a challenge to financial institutions' compliance divisions and possibly increase operating costs.[45] Financial institutions are also concerned about how B2V reform might impact the real estate sector, where the bulk of their loans and collateral reside.[46]

The B2V reform illustrates that SOEs are the elephant in the room in China's corporate tax reform. From a fiscal perspective, SOE reform would be beneficial on both sides of the ledger: the government could spend fewer of its fiscal resources subsidizing SOEs, while accruing additional revenue either by taxing SOEs directly or by letting private companies into sectors hitherto controlled by SOEs. So far, though, the only useful decision has been to require SOEs to distribute a larger portion of their profits back to the state in the form of dividends. The current dividend payout ratio ranges from 5 to 15 percent. In February 2013, the government announced a target to raise dividend ratios by another five percentage points by 2015.[47] The goal is for all SOEs to reach a 30 percent ratio by 2020.[48] If realized, the contribution to fiscal revenue would be considerable; some economists argue this is the *sine qua non* for bankrolling welfare payments.[49] But raising dividend payouts is not as good as privatizing SOEs and taxing their profits through formal fiscal legislation. As opposed to corporate tax evasion, it is difficult to imagine what legal actions the government can take if SOEs renege on dividend payouts.

At the other end of the spectrum, the government must decide how to tax the millions of small and medium-sized enterprises (SMEs) that now account for the majority of China's economic output. Economists at the Asian Development Bank have counseled China to find ways to increase the VAT, which could "enhance the neutrality and simplicity of the tax system" and provide a reliable base of funding for social welfare.[50] In July 2013, however, the State Council suspended the VAT and business tax for more than six million SMEs. These stimulus-driven tax cuts caused MOF to forego roughly RMB 12 billion ($2 billion) in tax revenue.[51] Such cuts, already undertaken during the global financial crisis, are an important reason why the VAT has declined as a share of tax revenue. SMEs might actually be better served by other economic measures, such as access to credit lines from state-owned banks.

[†††] China's telecommunications operators issued statements in June saying that B2V would lead to a significant decrease in their profits because the tax rate will rise from 3 percent (business tax) to 11 percent (VAT). Wei Tian, "Reform of Tax System with B2V Will Result in Winners and Losers," *China Daily*, July 30, 2014. *http://www.chinadaily.com.cn/business/2014-07/30/content_18207183.htm.*

Taxing Individuals: Hidden Wealth and the Burdened Middle Class

One of the oddities of China's tax system is that although Chinese households are earning better, the government is not keen to raise the personal income tax. In September 2011, MOF raised the monthly exemption threshold from individuals earning RMB 2,000 ($325) a month to those earning RMB 3,500 ($570). Effectively, 80 percent of China's taxpayers are not liable to pay personal income tax.[52] In the United States, only 43 percent of households do not pay federal income tax.[53] At a press conference in November 2013, Finance Minister Lou ruled out the possibility of raising the threshold again.[54] Still, several NPC delegates have proposed an even higher exemption threshold, with one citing a figure of RMB 6,000 to RMB 7,000.[55]

Why is the government acting against its fiscal self-interest? Political sensitivities may factor in. Beijing realizes that, unlike most authoritarian states, China is not a "windfall economy" that can export energy and redistribute the proceeds to its citizens. The decision in 2011 to raise the personal income tax exemption threshold coincided with a much-vaunted government campaign to combat inequality. The National Bureau of Statistics in February 2013 published the Gini coefficient for the first time since 2007, in order to appease critics who argued the Communist Party was not being candid about the nation's inequality crisis.[56] In parallel, it unveiled an ambitious plan to address income redistribution, which again included pledges to cut taxes for lower-income families.[‡‡‡]

Keeping income taxes low can also stimulate the economy. In theory, at least, it leaves the middle class with disposable income to spend. Low taxes can also woo corporate executives and wealthy individuals to China. At present, many prefer Hong Kong and Singapore for their lower tax rates, and exploit loopholes to have their paychecks issued there.[57]

And yet, these are not the only reasons why personal wealth is undertaxed in China. The fact is, ordinary Chinese feel their "tax burden," writ large, is heavy enough. The government has paid lip service to increasing "progressive" taxation on income, yet has not signaled an accompanying reduction in regressive taxes on consumption. Indeed, MOF intends to increase the tax rate on what it arbitrarily classifies as "luxury goods."[58] Taxes on energy-intensive goods and resources may sound like a good idea in principle, since millions of Chinese are suffering the consequences of pollution; yet such blanket taxes could result in higher household bills and consumer inflation, affecting the same income groups that suffer from regressive taxes.

Regressive taxes on consumption are particularly painful for families whose incomes have not kept pace with China's economic boom. Real wage growth is picking up, helped by low inflation, labor shortages, and government efforts to improve labor laws and the minimum wage. But the ratio of wages to GDP has declined to about 36 percent from 45 percent a decade ago.[59] Collective bargaining is circumscribed and income inequality is deepening.[60]

Middle-income Chinese might be open in principle to progressive income taxes or, for that matter, higher capital gains taxes and property taxes that prevent asset bubbles. Yet they also take into account what such taxes could do to their personal wealth. Capital and financial controls force households to deposit their limited earnings into bank accounts that offer zero to negative returns. There are strict limits on the funds that can be shifted

---

[‡‡‡] For more details on the February 2013 inequality reform plan, see Nargiza Salidjanova, *China's New Income Inequality Reform Plan and Implications for Rebalancing* (U.S.-China Economic and Security Review Commission, March 12, 2013). *http://origin.www.uscc.gov/sites/default/files/Research/China%20Inequality%20-%203%2012%2013.pdf.*

overseas, domestic stock markets are dismal, and pension and mutual funds have not yet been developed.[61] That makes property the primary source of nonmonetary wealth, offering an average annual inflation-adjusted return of 5 percent in 2007–2013.[62] The specter of higher taxes has already provoked extreme responses: when Beijing municipality introduced a 20 percent capital gains tax on the sale of second homes owned by married couples, divorce rates spiked as people scrambled to evade the tax.[63]

China's tax authorities also lack institutional capacity. China does not have a cohesive nationwide database to assess individual wealth and tax liabilities. The absence of such a database greatly facilitates tax evasion, and poses enormous technical barriers to levying taxes on nonwage income. Moreover, China's wage-based personal income tax practically precludes deductions. By contrast, the U.S. personal income tax allows individuals to make a number of deductions on their personal income statements, taking into account factors such as mortgage interest payments, child-rearing costs, and personal business expenses.

It is hard for ordinary Chinese people to see how their tax payments translate into social benefits. Like real wages, social expenditures are rising. But in 2012 a mere 30 percent of government revenue went toward social security, education, and healthcare, compared with an average of 52 percent in other middle-income countries.[64] It is common to pay fees and bribes to receive better schooling or medical treatment. Due to incomplete reform of the *hukou* system, migrant workers pay taxes in the city without reaping the social benefits. Scholars at Renmin University in Beijing have found that, due to different degrees of welfare spending in urban and rural areas, the "urban-rural Gini coefficient" for old age and medical spending is higher than for household income.[65] A study of urban incomes in Liaoning, a province in northeast China, found inequality actually increased after taxes were collected and revenues spent.[66]

The dearth of information on the wealthiest Chinese—many of whom are tied to the Party state—further undermines public confidence. Critics argue that the official Gini statistics China published in 2013 were massaged to gloss over deeper income fissures; alternative estimates are much higher (see Figure 5).[§§§] French economist Thomas Piketty's *Capital in the 21st Century*, a study of inequality in Western countries, would not be possible in China, where the tax returns Piketty uses to measure wealth distribution are inaccurate.[****] With the exception of individual cases (especially in Guangdong Province in 2012), Party cadres in China do not disclose their private wealth.[67] Using proxies such as real estate, travel, and luxury goods spending, Chinese scholar Wang Xiaolu finds billions of dollars in disguised income among China's top 10 percent of earners.[68]

[§§§] According to economists Nicholas Lardy and Nicholas Borst of the Peterson Institute for International Economics, "Innovative survey work done by the Southwest University of Finance and Economics in the China Household Finance Survey (CHFS) suggests that income inequality may be even higher than these estimates. If this survey's results are accurate, China's Gini coefficient in 2010 is actually .61, placing it amongst the most unequal countries in the world. The survey finds that the top 5 percent of households in China account for 62 percent of total savings. The bottom 55 percent of households have little or no savings. This is in stark contrast to the National Bureau of Statistics data, which show that even the second decile of earners in urban China are saving 20 percent of their income. According to the CHFS, those in the 90th percentile have an average saving rate of 61 percent and those in the 95th percentile save an average of 69 percent." Nicholas Lardy and Nicholas Borst, "A Blueprint for Rebalancing the Chinese Economy," *Peterson Policy Brief 13-02* (Peterson Institute for International Economics, February 2013), p. 7.

[****] See Thomas Piketty, *Capital in the 21st Century* (Cambridge, MA: The Belknap Press of Harvard University Press, 2014).

Figure 5: Gini Coefficients in China and Other Countries
(1 = maximum inequality)

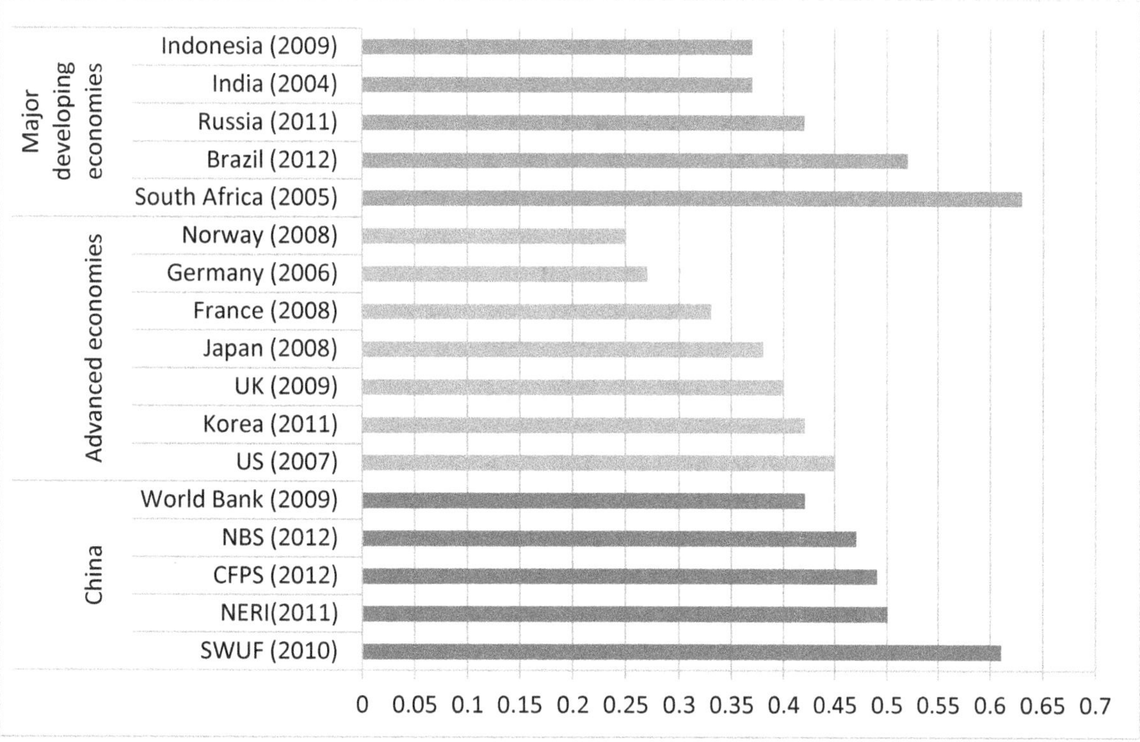

	Gini Coefficient
Major developing economies	
Indonesia (2009)	~0.37
India (2004)	~0.37
Russia (2011)	~0.42
Brazil (2012)	~0.52
South Africa (2005)	~0.63
Advanced economies	
Norway (2008)	~0.25
Germany (2006)	~0.27
France (2008)	~0.33
Japan (2008)	~0.38
UK (2009)	~0.40
Korea (2011)	~0.42
US (2007)	~0.45
China	
World Bank (2009)	~0.42
NBS (2012)	~0.47
CFPS (2012)	~0.49
NERI (2011)	~0.50
SWUF (2010)	~0.61

Horizontal axis: 0   0.05   0.1   0.15   0.2   0.25   0.3   0.35   0.4   0.45   0.5   0.55   0.6   0.65   0.7

Sources: World Bank, National Bureau of Statistics, media sources (for China estimates); CIA World Factbook (for all other countries).
Note: CFPS refers to China Family Planning Survey; NBS refers to National Bureau of Statistics; SWUF refers to Southwest University of Finance; and NERI refers to China National Economic Research Institute.

China's rich are funneling troves of personal wealth out of China. Common ruses include false invoicing of import and export receipts and gambling-related money laundering through Macau.[††††] A survey by Barclays bank, released in September 2014, showed nearly half of China's high-net-worth individuals (those with over $1.5 million in net assets) want to move abroad in the next five years, compared to 16 percent in Hong Kong, 6 percent in the United States, and 5 percent in India.[69]

Taxing Property and Resources: Market Cycles and Technical Barriers

China's efforts to tax property and resources are interrelated. Property drives the demand for resource-intensive industrial inputs such as steel, aluminum, glass, and cement. Building sprees on the outskirts of cities consume China's scarce arable land. Taxes that discourage property speculation could induce better use of resources; taxes based on the market price of resources, above all coal, would make property development costlier.

A common challenge for new levies on property and resources is that they add to a dense web of fees and taxes. It is doubtful whether the property tax currently proposed will

---

[††††] For more information on money laundering in Macau, see Chapter 3.3 of the *2013 USCC Annual Report*. http://origin.www.uscc.gov/sites/default/files/Annual_Report/Chapters/Chapter%203%3B%20Section%203%20Macau%20and%20Hong%20Kong.pdf.

actually eliminate land transfer fees and transaction-based property taxes at the local level.[‡‡‡‡] China certainly needs greater revenue to finance environmental cleanup efforts, yet its environment-related taxes and levies have tripled since 1994, and as a share of GDP are just below the OECD average.[70] For many property owners and energy-intensive producers, the existing burden is significant.

Market cycles are also pivotal in determining the desirability of taxes. The existing property taxes charged by local governments are popular when the housing market is booming, as it last did in 2012–2013 (see Figure 6). During upswings, such taxes (along with other measures, like financing restrictions on second homes) help deflate housing bubbles. When the housing market is in a downcycle, however, a property tax—especially the nationwide recurring tax currently on the table—suddenly becomes much less popular. Local governments, reliant on land as a source of tax revenue and as collateral for off-budget borrowing, worry about the decline in land and property values; banks worry about their outstanding assets; private individuals, holding about two-fifths of their wealth in housing, worry about their fortunes; and macroeconomic planners worry that a housing bust will cause the economy to unravel. Thus, the housing slump in 2014 may explain the government's hesitancy to introduce the recurring property tax.

Figure 6: Growth of Buildings Sold in China
(YTD monthly, year-on-year, %)

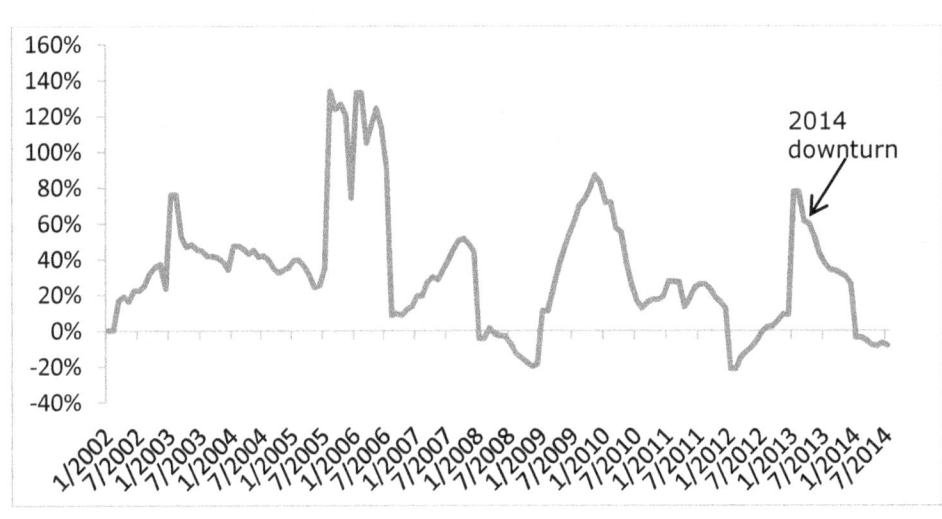

Source: China National Bureau of Statistics, via CEIC.

For resource taxes, market cycles have the opposite effect. When resource prices are high, an ad valorem tax—such as the one being proposed for coal—becomes costly. On the other hand, when prices are trending downward, an ad valorem tax is more palatable. As Figure 7 shows, the price of power coal in China has declined over the past two years. In the overall economy, producer price inflation is negative, and consumer inflation is at around 2

[‡‡‡‡] A total of 12 tax items are imposed on the development, sales, and holding sectors of the real estate industry. They include land value-added tax, deed tax, business tax, and corporate income tax. Various other fees are also imposed on the property sector; however, these do not include land transfer fees, a major component of government funds, which are not calculated as part of the public finance budget. Zhang Monan, a leading Chinese economist, has called for a unified property tax that combines the existing property tax, urban property tax, land use tax, land value increment tax, and land transfer fees. Zeng Yangpeng, "Local Govts' Fiscal Revenue Growth Slows," *China Daily*, August 8, 2013. *http://www.chinadaily.com.cn/bizchina/2013-08/08/content_16879833.htm*; Zhang Monan, "Tax Reform Needed to Pay Public Services," *China Daily*, March 13, 2013. *http://usa.chinadaily.com.cn/epaper/2013-03/13/content_16305019.htm*.

percent.[71] Still, a price-based resource tax could upset producers and consumers accustomed to low electricity prices.[72] In regions that host energy-intensive production, such as the northwest and northeast, the additional revenues accrued from the coal-based resource tax could come at the cost of overall economic growth.

Figure 7: Contract Price for Power Coal in China
(RMB/ton)

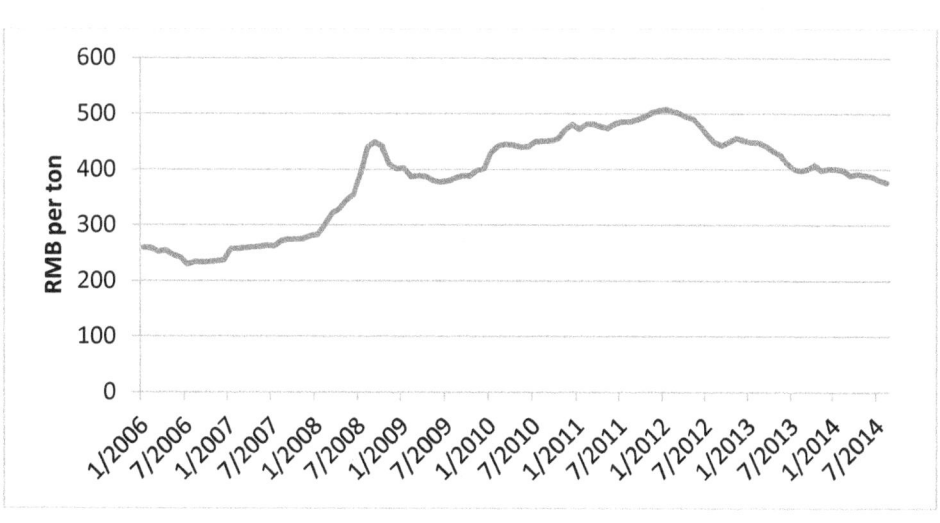

Source: China National Bureau of Statistics, via CEIC.
Note: Price at railway station; 4500-5000 calorie.

The government will need to create additional adjustments to make sophisticated property and resource taxes a success. China does not have a nationwide registration and valuation system for property holdings; preliminary efforts to create one have been harder than anticipated, and have exposed cases of corruption among public officials. The Chinese public has been appalled, for instance, by revelations that Zhao Haibin, a corrupt police chief in Guangdong Province, had amassed 192 properties using fake identification.[73] In the resource sector, the challenge is to establish a comprehensive framework of environmental regulation that fines polluters, reduces their access to bank credit, and incentivizes emissions reductions (potentially through a carbon tax). A tiered pricing model, currently being implemented in segments of the resource sector, could also ensure the costs of environmental externalities are spread along the industrial value chain, so as not to squeeze companies caught in the middle.

Beyond Tax Reform: Budget Management and Center-Local Relations

The Chinese government is aware that changing the tax code alone won't fix the fiscal system. Above all, it must address the relationship between MOF, central-level agencies, and local governments. Who gets to raise revenues from which taxes? Who determines and monitors how the revenues are spent? How can borrowing and transfers be used equitably and efficiently, without inducing waste and debt?

In some respects, Beijing has a well-articulated vision of what needs to be done. Based on statements made in the 2013 Third Plenum Decision and at the 2014 NPC meetings, the government's goals include:

- *Increasing budget transparency.* MOF will require most ministries to publish detailed budgets in 2014 and encourage local governments to begin doing the same. This is designed to avoid waste, especially lavish spending by high-level officials.[74]
- *Increasing budget flexibility.* Finance Minister Lou emphasized the annual budget revenue figures are not targets that must be met at all costs. The aim is to prevent local tax officials from squeezing local businesses to achieve their targets when the economy is weak (a "pro-cyclical bias"). In addition, MOF wants to depart from a system by which the NPC authorizes the government budget at its annual meetings each March, which preempts any major modifications during the rest of the year. Enhanced flexibility could optimize spending and saving based on the market cycle. One administrative solution being considered is to let the Economic and Finance Committee of the NPC sign off on budget adjustments throughout the year.[75]
- *Establishing a medium-term budget framework.* China only publishes an annual budget. The government will aim to establish a medium-term budget framework to ensure it can meet rising social spending commitments and gradually pay down local government debt. MOF will begin work on broad budgets to set out spending commitments three years into the future.[76]

The government has been reluctant, however, to clarify the distribution of fiscal power between the center and the localities. The Third Plenum Decision vaguely states that "authority" should be commensurate with "responsibility"—presumably, that agencies should have the budgetary resources they need to finance mandatory expenditures.[77] A latent uncertainty is how Beijing will discipline officials that accumulate off-budget debts, and also whether it will permit local governments to issue bonds independently. Last year's Third Plenum Decision signaled that Beijing will prevent promotion of Party cadres that mishandle local finances. A circular from the Communist Party's Organization Department, released weeks later, calls on cadres to be punished for decisions that "result in huge losses to the country."[78] In its March 2014 report to the NPC, MOF announced its intention to integrate LGFVs—hitherto independently operated outside Beijing's purview—into local government budgets.[79] By contrast, the National Development and Reform Commission, China's main industrial planning body (and staunch supporter of spending on infrastructure and industry), has said it would consider letting local governments roll over their debts in order to keep public projects running.[80]

MOF has loosened its monopoly on issuing government debt, but only moderately. Trials to sell municipal bonds were launched in 2011 in the cities of Shanghai and Shenzhen, as well as Zhejiang and Guangdong Provinces, and have extended to six other jurisdictions since then. The latest development came on August 31, 2014, when MOF announced that China's Budget Law had been amended to allow for limited bond issuances by local governments nationwide. Finance Minister Lou claimed the amendment would "solve the problem of borrowing money" for local governments.[81] In reality, though, local governments can only sell debt to invest in specific projects; bond sales to finance day-to-day expenditures remain prohibited, as are all forms of credit guarantees to individuals or entities.[82] In other words, China's provinces and municipalities are a long way from enjoying the debt-issuance rights of their counterparts in the United States.§§§§

---

§§§§ In the United States, tens of thousands of state and local governments issue bonds, primarily for public works. Projects that benefit the entire community are typically repaid by local tax revenue, while projects that benefit only select users (e.g., airport facilities) are typically repaid with fees collected from the users. Based on the 1913 federal income tax law, most municipal bonds are exempt from federal taxation. When bonds are issued to finance activities that do not provide significant benefit to the public, such as replenishing a municipality's underfunded pension plan, the federal government has the authority to tax the interest earned on those bonds. However, unlike in China, the U.S. federal government cannot prohibit state and local governments from issuing the bonds. Securities Industry and Financial Markets Association, "What You Should Know: The Role of Bonds in America."

Aside from borrowing rights, the government has not clarified whether it will give local governments a bigger slice of national tax revenue. Raising the local government share of national VAT revenue, for instance, could become a necessity, since the elimination of the business tax will deprive local governments of their largest source of tax revenue. The Third Plenum Decision, though, calls for "appropriately strengthening the authority and spending responsibility of the central government."[83] At the March NPC meetings, MOF announced it would crack down on local corporate and personal income tax rebates used to attract enterprises and high-net-worth individuals.[84] Finance Minister Lou has suggested that local governments may need State Council approval before granting such rebates.[85]

The future allocation of spending obligations is uncertain as well. The central government has pledged to realign transfer payments and assume a larger share of costs for transregional projects, but that says little about how it will help municipal governments finance soaring welfare costs.[86] Those who support local governments argue that Beijing should assume greater responsibility for providing social services such as education, healthcare, and pensions, whether through direct spending or transfer increases.[87] Others contend local governments could do a better job of managing their existing resources. For example, Jia Kang, director of the influential Research Institute of Fiscal Science at MOF, calls for improving the functions and purpose of lower levels of government to avoid wasteful spending.[88]

Regardless which way the axe falls on revenue and spending, there will be no "one size fits all" remedy for China's diverse localities. While MOF wants local governments to raise progressive taxes on personal income, their ability to do so varies widely. A 2012 analysis published by *CNN*, for example, found half of China's millionaires reside in just three jurisdictions: Beijing (18 percent), Guangdong (17 percent), and Shanghai (15 percent).[89] A survey of local budgets in four places—Chongqing, Beijing, Jiangsu, and Anhui—also demonstrates the diversity of the local tax base (Figures 8.1 and 8.2). While all of these jurisdictions rely on business and VAT taxes, Beijing extracts major fiscal resources from enterprises; Chongqing and Jiangsu rely heavily on land- and housing-related taxes; and Anhui, a poor inland region, collects a miscellany of other taxes.

Analysis of China's provinces, municipalities, and autonomous regions also shows the importance of nontax revenue varies widely (see Figure 9). Chongqing, notorious for its housing bubbles and use of property-based debt financing, leads the nation in nontax budget revenue, at 43 percent. Some other provinces are not far behind. Higher-income provinces tend to have less nontax revenue, yet there are exceptions (e.g., Tianjin municipality).

www.investinginbonds.com/learnmore.asp?catid=3&id=50;   Fidelity,   "Municipal   Bonds."
https://www.fidelity.com/fixed-income-bonds/individual-bonds/municipal-bonds.

Figure 8.1: Breakdown of Tax Revenue in Chongqing and Beijing Municipalities, 2012 (share, %)

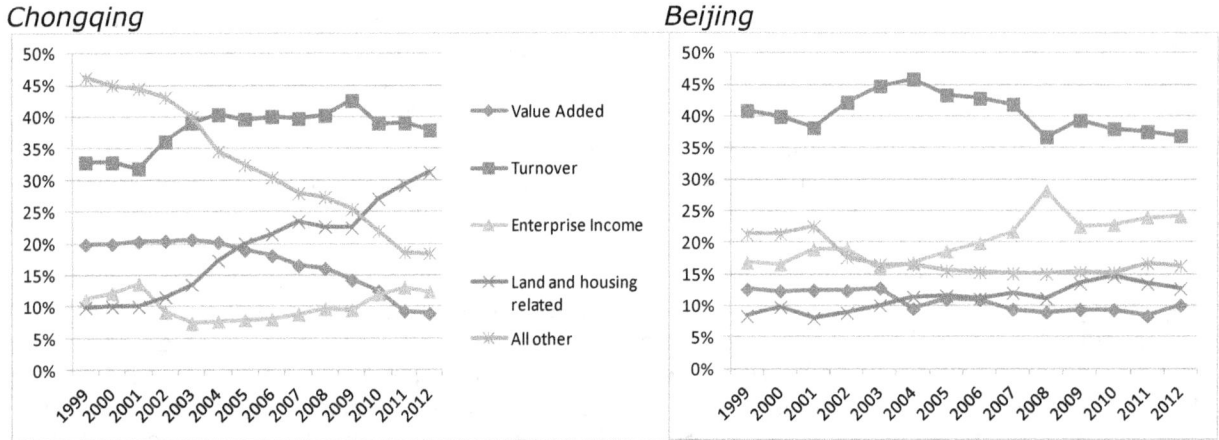

Source: China's Ministry of Finance, via CEIC.

Figure 8.2: Breakdown of Tax Revenue in Jiangsu and Anhui Provinces, 2012 (share, %)

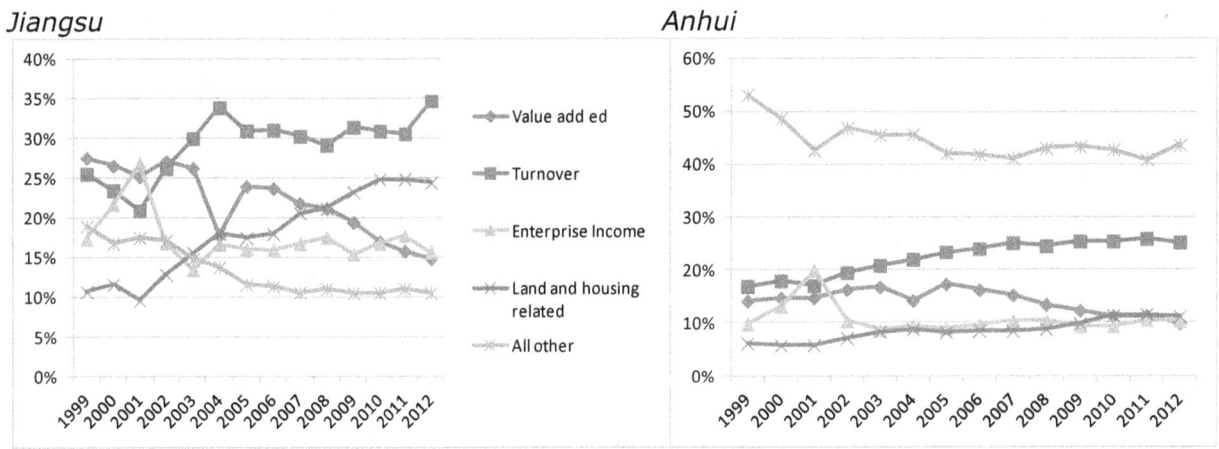

Source: China's Ministry of Finance, via CEIC.

Figure 9: Non-Tax Share of Provincial Fiscal Revenue, 2012
(share, %)

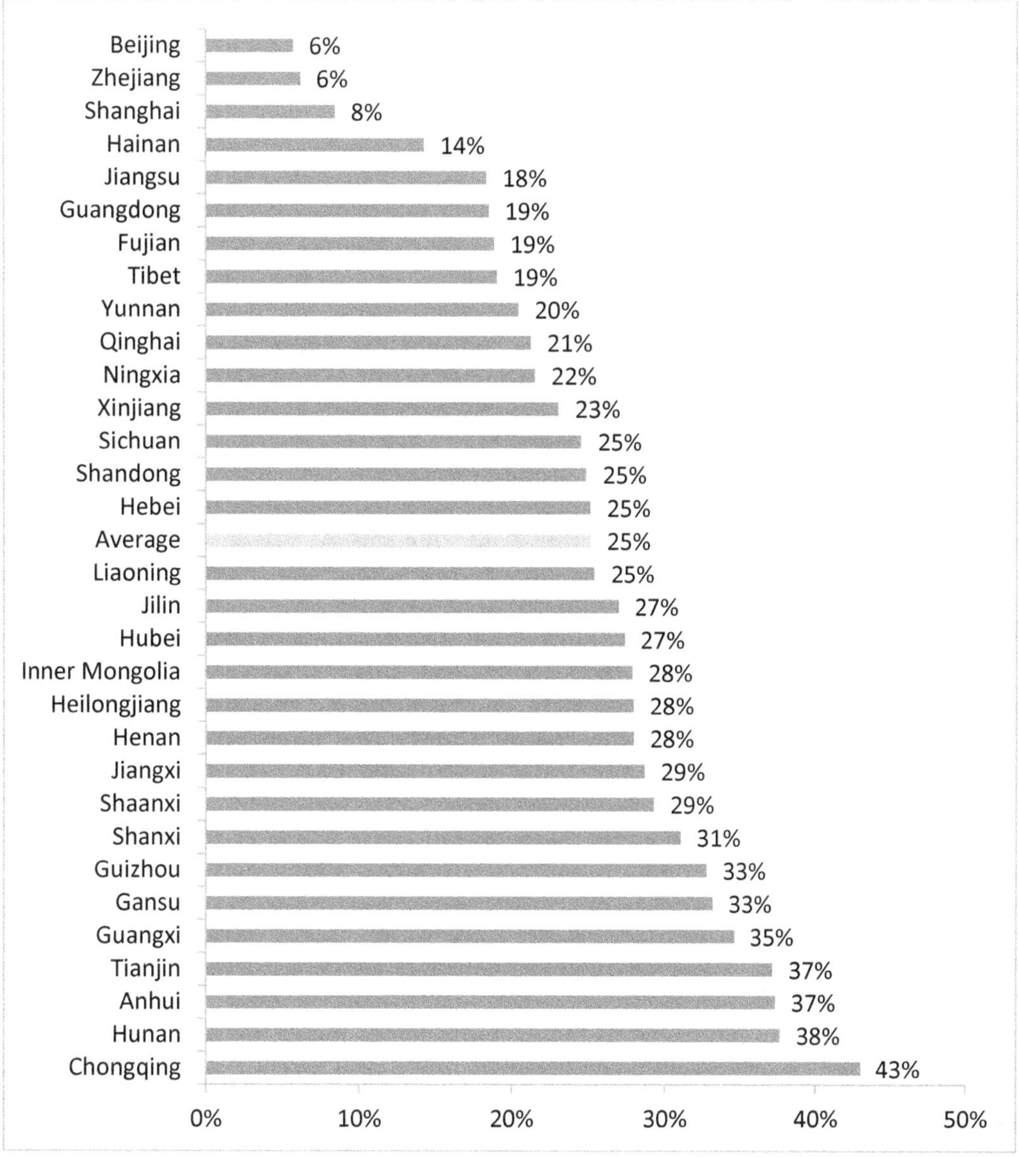

Province	Share (%)
Beijing	6%
Zhejiang	6%
Shanghai	8%
Hainan	14%
Jiangsu	18%
Guangdong	19%
Fujian	19%
Tibet	19%
Yunnan	20%
Qinghai	21%
Ningxia	22%
Xinjiang	23%
Sichuan	25%
Shandong	25%
Hebei	25%
Average	25%
Liaoning	25%
Jilin	27%
Hubei	27%
Inner Mongolia	28%
Heilongjiang	28%
Henan	28%
Jiangxi	29%
Shaanxi	29%
Shanxi	31%
Guizhou	33%
Gansu	33%
Guangxi	35%
Tianjin	37%
Anhui	37%
Hunan	38%
Chongqing	43%

Source: China's Ministry of Finance, via CEIC.

Political dynamics will continue to impede fiscal reform in China. The central government will have a difficult time severing the deep ties between local governments and SOEs, or preventing the inter-regional "fiscal wars" that have shaped China's economic model since the 1980s. Cutting-edge research, published in the *American Political Science Review*, shows fiscal extraction in China increases when more Party officials at the county level are forced to compete for promotion at the prefecture level. Faced with a paucity of fiscal resources to implement unfunded mandates, the officials signal political loyalty and competence by levying excessive taxes and fees on the local population.[*****]

Implications for the United States

U.S. businesses operating in China have publicly supported the country's tax reforms, as statements by the American Chamber of Commerce indicate.[90] They hope China one day can emulate the more streamlined tax systems of advanced economies. At the same time, Beijing's "heavier fiscal touch"—beginning with a higher corporate income tax in 2008—also adds to the rising cost of doing business in China. Preventing local governments from offering tax breaks may be good policy, yet it will reduce the leeway for U.S. companies to shop around for the best tax subsidies. Foreign companies appear to support China's switch from a business to a value-added tax on services, yet the phased rollout of this reform has provoked divergent responses across industries.[†††††] All the while, China has shown few signs of giving up other tax policies that harm U.S. companies—from tax breaks for SOEs to discriminatory taxes on imports of U.S. goods.

Fiscal reform could accelerate the rebalancing of China's economy and correct the deep imbalances in U.S.-China economic relations. At this stage, however, few measures have actually been implemented, and it is too early to tell where the leadership's priorities lie. Is Beijing primarily seeking to raise revenue to cope with an aging population and overcome the debt "hangover" of the 2009 stimulus? Or is fiscal reform nothing more than a power grab by the new leadership? Or is there an intrinsic interest in using taxes to reform the economy? If resource taxes hurt consumers or the property market deteriorates, will MOF steer a different course? Even if the will is there, the government must develop the technical wherewithal to implement sophisticated tax policies.

[*****] The authors, Xiaobo Lü (University of Texas) and Pierre F. Landry (University of Pittsburgh), argue the more counties there are in a prefecture, the more county-level officials compete for a higher post in the Chinese government. Fiscal extraction rises along with political competition as cadres use their ability to fund mandates and generate revenue to stand out among their peers. The authors measure extraction in terms of intensity (log of taxation per capita) and level (taxation as a share of local GDP). The link between fiscal competition and political competition holds even when taking into account other factors such as local economic features and endowments. Xiaobo Lü and Pierre F. Landry, "Show Me the Money: Interjurisdiction Political Competition and Fiscal Extraction in China," *American Political Science Review* 108:3 (August 2014): 706-722.

[†††††] In the 2014 member survey of the European Union Chamber of Commerce, 58 percent of respondents said they were unsure as to whether B2V reform can benefit their company. European Union Chamber of Commerce in China, *Business Confidence Survey 2014* (Beijing, China), pp. 41-42.

[1] MNI, "China Politburo Aims to Finish Major Fiscal Reforms by 2016," June 30, 2014. *https://mninews.marketnews.com/content/china-politburo-aims-finish-major-fiscal-reforms-2016*.

[2] *China Daily,* "China Banking on Tax Reforms to Help Transform," August 26, 2013. *http://www.chinadaily.com.cn/business/2013-08/26/content_16920401.htm*.

[3] Ehtisham Ahmad, Li Keping, and Thomas Richardson, "Recentralization in China?" (Washington, DC: International Monetary Fund, November 2002). *https://www.imf.org/external/pubs/ft/seminar/2000/fiscal/ahmad.pdf*.

[4] *China Daily,* "China Banking on Tax Reforms to Help Transform," August 26, 2013. *http://www.chinadaily.com.cn/business/2013-08/26/content_16920401.htm*.

[5] Zhang Monan, "Tax Reform Needed to Pay Public Services," *China Daily*, March 13, 2013. *http://usa.chinadaily.com.cn/epaper/2013-03/13/content_16305019.htm*.

[6] Wei Tian, "More Tax Reforms on Agenda: Minister," *China Daily*, March 7, 2014. *http://www.chinadaily.com.cn/business/2014-03/07/content_17329196.htm*.

[7] *How China Restructure its Tax System: Q&A with Wei Xiong [Professor of Law at Wuhan University]* (Max Planck Institute for Tax Law and Public Finance, October 2013). *http://www.tax.mpg.de/en/pub/news/chinese_tax_reforms.cfm*.

[8] Takehiko Nakao [President of Asian Development Bank], "The Road to Public Finance Reform" (Speech delivered at China Development Forum 2014, Beijing, March 23, 2014) reprinted by *China Daily*, March 25, 2014. *http://www.chinadaily.com.cn/business/2014-03/25/content_17377356.htm*.

[9] Shaoguang Wang and Angang Hu, *The Political Economy of Uneven Development: The Case of China* (New York, NY: ME Sharpe, 1999), pp. 1-17; Xiaobo Lü and Pierre F. Landry, "Show Me the Money: Interjurisdiction Political Competition and Fiscal Extraction in China," *American Political Science Review* 108:3 (August 2014): 720.

[10] Jean C. Oi, "Fiscal Reform and the Economic Foundations of Local State Corporatism in China." *World Politics* 45:1 (1992): 99–126; Shaoguang Wang, "China's 1994 Fiscal Reform: An Initial Assessment," *Asian Survey* 37:9 (1997): 801–817.

[11] Nicholas Lardy, *Sustaining China's Economic Growth after the Global Financial Crisis* (Peterson Institution for International Economics, 2012), pp. 69-70.

[12] *China Daily*, "No Hasty Tax Reforms," March 11, 2014. *http://www.chinadaily.com.cn/business/2014-03/11/content_17337208.htm*.

[13] *Financial Times*, "China's Dangerous Credit Addiction," January 15, 2014. *http://www.ft.com/cms/s/0/3a5de202-7ddf-11e3-b409-00144feabdc0.html#axzz3ELqiDuDk*.

[14] Takehiko Nakao [President of Asian Development Bank], "The Road to Public Finance Reform" (Speech delivered at China Development Forum 2014, Beijing, March 23, 2014) reprinted by *China Daily*, March 25, 2014. *http://www.chinadaily.com.cn/business/2014-03/25/content_17377356.htm*.

[15] *Financial Times*, "China's Dangerous Credit Addiction," January 15, 2014. *http://www.ft.com/cms/s/0/3a5de202-7ddf-11e3-b409-00144feabdc0.html#axzz3ELqiDuDk*.

[16] Bloomberg, "China Pledges to Tackle Local Government Debt amid Reform," December 13, 2013. *http://www.bloomberg.com/news/2013-12-13/china-pledges-to-tackle-local-government-debt-amid-reform-push.html*.

[17] Bloomberg, "China's Local Debt Swells to 17.9 Trillion Yuan in Audit," December 30, 2013. *http://www.bloomberg.com/news/2013-12-30/china-s-local-debt-swells-to-17-9-trillion-yuan-in-audit.html*.

[18] Bloomberg, "China's Local Debt Swells to 17.9 Trillion Yuan in Audit," December 30, 2013. *http://www.bloomberg.com/news/2013-12-30/china-s-local-debt-swells-to-17-9-trillion-yuan-in-audit.html*.

[19] *Full Text of Li Keqiang's Government Work Report at 2nd Session of 12th NPC* (Beijing, China), *CCTV-1*, March 5, 2014. Hosted by Open Source Center. ID: CHO2014030429060374.

[20] Takehiko Nakao [President of Asian Development Bank], "The Road to Public Finance Reform" (Speech delivered at China Development Forum 2014, Beijing, March 23, 2014) reprinted by *China Daily*, March 25, 2014. *http://www.chinadaily.com.cn/business/2014-03/25/content_17377356.htm*.

[21] *Economist*, September 6, 2014, p. 96.

[22] *China Daily,* "China Banking on Tax Reforms to Help Transform," August 26, 2013. *http://www.chinadaily.com.cn/business/2013-08/26/content_16920401.htm*.

[23] Stephen Green, "Chinese Finance Minister's To-Do List," *China Daily*, March 7, 2014. *http://www.chinadaily.com.cn/business/2014-03/07/content_17331598.htm*.

[24] Data from China's Ministry of Finance, via CEIC data.

[25] Zeng Yangpeng, "Local Govts' Fiscal Revenue Growth Slows," *China Daily*, August 8, 2013. *http://www.chinadaily.com.cn/bizchina/2013-08/08/content_16879833.htm.*

[26] Karen Eggleston et al., "Will Demographic Change Slow China's Rise?" *Journal of Asian Studies* 72:3 (August 2013): 505.

[27] Lan Lan, "Reliance on Land Sales 'Must Be Reformed'," *China Daily*, January 7, 2013, via Factiva.

[28] U.S.-China Economic and Security Review Commission, *Hearing on China's Healthcare Sector, Drug Safety, and the U.S.-China Trade in Medical Products*, testimony of Yanzhong Huang, April 3, 2014.

[29] Xinhua (English edition), *Full Text of 8th CPC Central Committee Third Plenum Communiqué*, November 12, 2013. Hosted by Open Source Center. ID: CHR2013111248844920.

[30] Stephen Green, "Chinese Finance Minister's To-Do List," *China Daily*, March 7, 2014. *http://www.chinadaily.com.cn/business/2014-03/07/content_17331598.htm.*

[31] Carlos Tejada and MinJung Kim, "Beijing Plans to Spend $2.45 Trillion This Year. Here's How," *Wall Street Journal – China Real Time* (Blog), March 5, 2014. *http://blogs.wsj.com/chinarealtime/2014/03/05/beijing-plans-to-spend-2-45-trillion-this-year-heres-how/.*

[32] Zeng Yangpeng, "Local Govts' Fiscal Revenue Growth Slows," *China Daily*, August 8, 2013. *http://www.chinadaily.com.cn/bizchina/2013-08/08/content_16879833.htm.*

[33] Robert Wihtol and Yolanda Fernandez Lommen, "Income Distribution Is the Key," *China Daily*, October 30, 2012. *http://usa.chinadaily.com.cn/opinion/2012-10/30/content_15855526.htm.*

[34] Xinhua (English edition), "Coal, Electricity Prices Expected to Rise," *China Daily*, July 3, 2014. *http://www.chinadaily.com.cn/business/2014-07/03/content_17641628.htm.*

[35] Ryan Rutkowski, "Rebalancing China's Tax Policy" (Paper presented at symposium on The U.S.-China-Europe Economic Reform Agenda, Beijing, China, May 17-18, 2014), pp. 19-20; *China Daily*, "More Sectors Added to VAT-Reform Program," May 29, 2013, via Factiva; Wei Tian, "Reform of Tax System with B2V Will Result in Winners and Losers," *China Daily*, July 30, 2014. *http://www.chinadaily.com.cn/business/2014-07/30/content_18207183.htm.*

[36] Wei Tian, "Reform of Tax System with B2V Will Result in Winners and Losers," *China Daily*, July 30, 2014. *http://www.chinadaily.com.cn/business/2014-07/30/content_18207183.htm.*

[37] Ryan Rutkowski, "Rebalancing China's Tax Policy" (Paper presented at symposium on The U.S.-China-Europe Economic Reform Agenda, Beijing, China, May 17-18, 2014), p. 22.

[38] Stephen Green, "Chinese Finance Minister's To-Do List," *China Daily*, March 7, 2014. *http://www.chinadaily.com.cn/business/2014-03/07/content_17331598.htm*; Ryan Rutkowski, "Rebalancing China's Tax Policy" (Paper presented at symposium on The U.S.-China-Europe Economic Reform Agenda, Beijing, China, May 17-18, 2014), pp.24-25.

[39] Ryan Rutkowski, "Rebalancing China's Tax Policy" (Paper presented at symposium on The U.S.-China-Europe Economic Reform Agenda, Beijing, China, May 17-18, 2014), p. 27.

[40] Xinhua (English edition), *Full Text of 8th CPC Central Committee Third Plenum Communiqué*, November 12, 2013. Hosted by Open Source Center. ID: CHR2013111248844920.

[41] *Economist* Intelligence Unit, "China: Tax Regulations," February 28, 2013, via Factiva.

[42] Data from China's Ministry of Finance, via CEIC data.

[43] Ryan Rutkowski, "Rebalancing China's Tax Policy" (Paper presented at symposium on The U.S.-China-Europe Economic Reform Agenda, Beijing, China, May 17-18, 2014), pp. 19-22; *China Daily*, "China Banking on Tax Reforms to Help Transform," August 26, 2013. *http://www.chinadaily.com.cn/business/2013-08/26/content_16920401.htm.*

[44] Wei Tian, "Reform of Tax System with B2V Will Result in Winners and Losers," *China Daily*, July 30, 2014. *http://www.chinadaily.com.cn/business/2014-07/30/content_18207183.htm.*

[45] Wei Tian, "Reform of Tax System with B2V Will Result in Winners and Losers," *China Daily*, July 30, 2014. *http://www.chinadaily.com.cn/business/2014-07/30/content_18207183.htm.*

[46] Ryan Rutkowski, "Rebalancing China's Tax Policy" (Paper presented at symposium on The U.S.-China-Europe Economic Reform Agenda, Beijing, China, May 17-18, 2014), p. 22.

[47] *Economist* Intelligence Unit, "China Regulations: A House Divided," February 9, 2013, via Factiva.

[48] Xinhua (English edition), *Full Text of 8th CPC Central Committee Third Plenum Communiqué*, November 12, 2013. Hosted by Open Source Center. ID: CHR2013111248844920.

[49] Takehiko Nakao [President of Asian Development Bank], "The Road to Public Finance Reform" (Speech delivered at China Development Forum 2014, Beijing, March 23, 2014) reprinted by *China Daily*, March 25, 2014. *http://www.chinadaily.com.cn/business/2014-03/25/content_17377356.htm.*

[50] Takehiko Nakao [President of Asian Development Bank], "The Road to Public Finance Reform" (Speech delivered at China Development Forum 2014, Beijing, March 23, 2014) reprinted by *China Daily*, March 25, 2014. *http://www.chinadaily.com.cn/business/2014-03/25/content_17377356.htm*.

[51] Chen Jia, "Slowdown Curtails Tax Income," *China Daily*, July 30, 2013. *http://www.chinadaily.com.cn/cndy/2013-07/30/content_16849935.htm*.

[52] Yang Guoying, "The Dialectics of China's Tax Burden," *China Daily*, March 4, 2014, *http://www.chinadaily.com.cn/business/2014-03/04/content_17321215.htm*.

[53] Allison Linn, "Now It's the 43 Percent: Fewer Paying No Income Tax," CNBC, September 9, 2013. *http://www.cnbc.com/id/101015065#*.

[54] Wei Tian, "More Tax Reforms on Agenda: Minister," *China Daily*, March 7, 2014. *http://www.chinadaily.com.cn/business/2014-03/07/content_17329196.htm*.

[55] *China Daily*, "No Hasty Tax Reforms," March 11, 2014. *http://www.chinadaily.com.cn/business/2014-03/11/content_17337208.htm*.

[56] *China Daily*, "China Publishes Gini Coefficient's Measurements," February 2, 2013. *http://www.chinadaily.com.cn/business/2013-02/02/content_16195592.htm*.

[57] *China Daily*, "No Hasty Tax Reforms," March 11, 2014. *http://www.chinadaily.com.cn/business/2014-03/11/content_17337208.htm*.

[58] Langi Chiang and Jonathan Standing, "China May Tax More Luxury Goods, Expand Property Tax: Xinhua," Reuters, August 28, 2013. *http://www.reuters.com/article/2013/08/28/us-china-tax-idUSBRE97R0C420130828*.

[59] Robert Wihtol and Yolanda Fernandez Lommen, "Income Distribution Is the Key," *China Daily*, October 30, 2012. *http://usa.chinadaily.com.cn/opinion/2012-10/30/content_15855526.htm*.

[60] Gordon G. Chang, "College Grads Are Jobless in China's 'High-Growth' Economy," *Forbes*, May 26, 2013. *http://www.forbes.com/sites/gordonchang/2013/05/26/college-grads-are-jobless-in-chinas-high-growth-economy/*.

[61] Robert Wihtol and Yolanda Fernandez Lommen, "Income Distribution Is the Key," *China Daily*, October 30, 2012. *http://usa.chinadaily.com.cn/opinion/2012-10/30/content_15855526.htm*.

[62] Ryan Rutkowski, "Rebalancing China's Tax Policy" (Paper presented at symposium on The U.S.-China-Europe Economic Reform Agenda, Beijing, China, May 17-18, 2014), p. 25.

[63] Esther Fung, "Finance Minister: Divorce-Inducing Property Tax Is 'Defective'," *Wall Street Journal – China Real Time* (Blog), March 6, 2014. *http://blogs.wsj.com/chinarealtime/2014/03/06/finance-minister-divorce-inducing-property-tax-is-defective/*.

[64] Robert Wihtol and Yolanda Fernandez Lommen, "Income Distribution Is the Key," *China Daily*, October 30, 2012. *http://usa.chinadaily.com.cn/opinion/2012-10/30/content_15855526.htm*.

[65] Gu Haibin, Zhang Shitong, and Zhang Anjun, "Method and Evaluation of Urban-Rural Social Security Evenness in China," *Caijing Jingji* [Finance & Trade Economics] 11 (2012): 37-47 [Chinese translation].

[66] Zhao Guizhi, Ma Shucai, and Li Junhao, "The Financial Impact of Changes in the Income Gap and Policy Implications: The Case of Liaoning Urban Residents," *Jingji Wenti* [Economic Issues] 10 (2012): 115-118 [Chinese translation].

[67] Jun Ma, Lin Li, and Audrey Shi, "China Strategy: Reforms after Leadership Transition" (Beijing, China: Deutsche Bank, November 2012), p. 26.

[68] Wang Xiaolu, "The Current Status, Trends, and Reform Initiatives Regarding Income Distribution in China," *Zhongguo Shichang* [China Market] 20 (2010): 8-19. See also Iacob Koch-Weser, *The Reliability of China's Economic Data: An Analysis of National Output* (U.S.-China Economic and Security Review Commission, January 2013).

[69] James Griffiths, "Exodus of the Super-Rich: Half of China's Millionaires 'Plan to Leave Country within Five Years," *South China Morning Post*, September 15, 2014. *http://www.scmp.com/news/china/article/1592975/47-cent-chinese-super-rich-want-leave-country-barclays-survey*.

[70] Ryan Rutkowski, "Rebalancing China's Tax Policy" (Paper presented at symposium on The U.S.-China-Europe Economic Reform Agenda, Beijing, China, May 17-18, 2014), p. 22.

[71] Data from *Trading Economics*. *http://www.tradingeconomics.com/china/consumer-price-index-cpi*.

[72] Wei Tian, "Reform of Tax System with B2V Will Result in Winners and Losers," *China Daily*, July 30, 2014. *http://www.chinadaily.com.cn/business/2014-07/30/content_18207183.htm*.

[73] Esther Fung, "China Hit by Scandals over Officials' Property," *Wall Street Journal*, February 5, 2013. *http://blogs.wsj.com/corruption-currents/2013/02/05/china-hit-by-scandals-over-officials-property/*.

[74] Stephen Green, "Chinese Finance Minister's To-Do List," *China Daily*, March 7, 2014. *http://www.chinadaily.com.cn/business/2014-03/07/content_17331598.htm.*

[75] Stephen Green, "Chinese Finance Minister's To-Do List," *China Daily*, March 7, 2014. *http://www.chinadaily.com.cn/business/2014-03/07/content_17331598.htm.*

[76] Stephen Green, "Chinese Finance Minister's To-Do List," *China Daily*, March 7, 2014. *http://www.chinadaily.com.cn/business/2014-03/07/content_17331598.htm*; Third Plenum Decision.

[77] Xinhua (English edition), *Full Text of 8th CPC Central Committee Third Plenum Communiqué*, November 12, 2013. Hosted by Open Source Center. ID: CHR2013111248844920.

[78] Bloomberg, "China Pledges to Tackle Local Government Debt amid Reform," December 13, 2013. *http://www.bloomberg.com/news/2013-12-13/china-pledges-to-tackle-local-government-debt-amid-reform-push.html.*

[79] Stephen Green, "Chinese Finance Minister's To-Do List," *China Daily*, March 7, 2014. *http://www.chinadaily.com.cn/business/2014-03/07/content_17331598.htm.*

[80] Simon Rabinovich, "China Gives Local Government Go-ahead to Roll Over Debt," *Financial Times*, January 2, 2014. *http://www.ft.com/intl/cms/s/0/055e48f8-7371-11e3-a0c0-00144feabdc0.html#axzz3ELqiDuDk.*

[81] Bloomberg, "China Eases Rules on Bond Sales by Local Governments," August 31, 2014. *http://www.bloomberg.com/news/2014-08-31/china-eases-rules-on-bond-sales-by-local-governments.html.*

[82] Bloomberg, "China Eases Rules on Bond Sales by Local Governments," August 31, 2014. *http://www.bloomberg.com/news/2014-08-31/china-eases-rules-on-bond-sales-by-local-governments.html.*

[83] Xinhua (English edition), *Full Text of 8th CPC Central Committee Third Plenum Communiqué*, November 12, 2013. Hosted by Open Source Center. ID: CHR2013111248844920.

[84] Stephen Green, "Chinese Finance Minister's To-Do List," *China Daily*, March 7, 2014. *http://www.chinadaily.com.cn/business/2014-03/07/content_17331598.htm.*

[85] Wei Tian, "Reform of Tax System with B2V Will Result in Winners and Losers," *China Daily*, July 30, 2014. *http://www.chinadaily.com.cn/business/2014-07/30/content_18207183.htm.*

[86] Xinhua (English edition), *Full Text of 8th CPC Central Committee Third Plenum Communiqué*, November 12, 2013. Hosted by Open Source Center. ID: CHR2013111248844920.

[87] Takehiko Nakao [President of Asian Development Bank], "The Road to Public Finance Reform" (Speech delivered at China Development Forum 2014, Beijing, March 23, 2014) reprinted by *China Daily*, March 25, 2014. *http://www.chinadaily.com.cn/business/2014-03/25/content_17377356.htm.*

[88] *China Daily,* "China Banking on Tax Reforms to Help Transform," August 26, 2013 *http://www.chinadaily.com.cn/bizchina/2013-08/26/content_16920401.htm.*

[89] Charles Riley, "China Adds Fewer Millionaires as Economy Slows," *CNN Money*, August 16, 2013. *http://money.cnn.com/2013/08/16/news/china-wealth/index.html.*

[90] *Economist* Intelligence Unit, "China: Tax Regulations," February 28, 2013, via Factiva.

www.ingramcontent.com/pod-product-compliance
Lightning Source LLC
Chambersburg PA
CBHW080803290526

45790CB00008B/3571